H.J. TIDY

A COLLECTION OF
T R U E
PARANORMAL
POLICE ENCOUNTERS

Ghosts, Hauntings, and the Unknown

© **Copyright 2023 – H.J. Tidy All rights reserved.**

In no way is it legal to reproduce, duplicate, or transmit any part of this document in either electronic means or in printed format. Recording of this publication is strictly prohibited and any storage of this document is not allowed unless with written permission from the publisher. All rights reserved.

The information provided herein is stated to be truthful and consistent, in that any liability, in terms of inattention or otherwise, by any usage or abuse of any policies, processes, or directions contained within is the solitary and utter responsibility of the recipient reader. Under no circumstances will any legal responsibility or blame be held against the publisher for any reparation, damages, or monetary loss due to the information herein, either directly or indirectly.

Respective authors own all copyrights not held by the publisher.

Legal Notice:

This book is copyright protected. This is only for personal use. You cannot amend, distribute, sell, use, quote or paraphrase any part or the content within this book without the consent of the author or copyright owner. Legal action will be pursued if this is breached.

Fiction

This novel is entirely a work of fiction. The names, characters and incidents portrayed in it are the work of the author's imagination. Any resemblance to actual persons, living or dead, events or localities is entirely coincidental.

Disclaimer Notice:

Please note the information contained within this document is for educational and entertainment purposes only. Every attempt has been made to provide accurate, up to date and reliable complete information. No warranties of any kind are expressed or implied. Readers acknowledge that the author is not engaging in the rendering of legal, financial, medical or professional advice.

By reading this document, the reader agrees that under no circumstances are we responsible for any losses, direct or indirect, which are incurred as a result of the use of information contained within this document, including, but not limited to, −errors, omissions, or inaccuracies.

Moral rights

H.J. Tidy asserts the moral right to be identified as the author of this work.

External Content

H.J. Tidy has no responsibility for the persistence or accuracy of URLs for external or third-party Internet Websites referred to in this publication and does not guarantee that any content on such Websites is, or will remain, accurate or appropriate.

TABLE OF CONTENTS

INTRODUCTION v

THE NIGHT SHIFT 1

ENIGMA IN LOUISIANA 9

THE DORMITORY OF SECRETS 17

CHAPEL'S HAUNTING 25

PHOTOGRAPHIC MALEVOLENCE 31

NIGHTMARE PATROL 41

THE LANDLORD 49

CORNER HOUSE 55

THE NIGHT WATCH 61

 THE LIGHTHOUSE 69

PHANTOM FROLICKER 79

CASINO ENCOUNTER 85

CONCLUSION 93

INTRODUCTION

WITHIN THE ENIGMATIC REALM, where the commonplace merges with the eerie, we often encounter unsuspecting individuals thrust into spine-tingling encounters. Within the realm of the supernatural narrative, a conventional police officer might not initially appear as the archetypal hero. Amidst the mysterious tapestry of the unknown, a collection of unsettling tales emerges. These narratives detail moments when law enforcement officers faced inexplicable forces that challenged the limits of conventional understanding.

Envision this scenario: guardians of the law, vigilant sentinels of the night, enmeshed in perplexing and inexplicable incidents during their sworn duties. These are not fanciful tales spun from deceitful imaginations; they are the straightforward chronicles of those carrying badges. The narratives they recount have an undeniable aura of authenticity, sending shivers down the spine as they unravel the eerie threads that connect the guardians of order to the enigmatic and uncharted realms encountered in the line of duty.

Brace yourself for a collection of twelve mysterious tales that peel back the layers of perplexing encounters. As the trajectories of patrol paths cross and conventional careers are forsaken, a seamless amalgamation of law enforcement and the supernatural unfolds. Within these narratives lies a clandestine realm of peculiar secrets, shielded by officers whose experiences defy logical explanation. Step into a world where the boundaries between the earthly and otherworldly blur, revealing a tapestry of enigmatic stories woven by those who navigate the intersection of the tangible and the inexplicable.

This narrative isn't designed to persuade skeptics; it intends to captivate and mesmerize readers with genuine tales of individuals dwelling on the subtle boundary between the visible and the unseen. Delving into real people's lives and encounters, each story possesses a unique and haunting allure that transcends conventional boundaries.

Certain narratives within may contain chilling elements such as murder, suicide, and unsettling emotions. So, reader discretion is advised.

Embark on a chilling odyssey as we peel back the layers of spectral remnants lingering within the confines of a once-menacing hospital. Plunge into the foreboding depths of a dark swamp, shrouded in the tragedies of ages past. We meticulously unravel the veiled history of a university housing complex in the heart of a quaint Ohio town. Embark on disconcerting patrols alongside Officer Blake Munoz through the haunting precincts of an Ohio church complex, where a seasoned Crime Scene Photographer becomes ensnared in unsettling mysteries. Join us in documenting Officer Tony Hansen's fateful night in the enigmatic town of Salem, Massachusetts, and explore many other spine-tingling tales.

Each narrative provides a distinct perspective on the unexplainable, showcasing the courage of those who patrol the boundary between the known and the supernatural. Step into the shoes of these individuals as they navigate realms where the inexplicable becomes an integral part of their duty, illuminating the bravery required to confront the enigmatic forces that lurk beyond the visible.

Prepare for a thrilling journey into the supernatural, where the mysterious seamlessly blends with the ordinary in tales that will linger in the depths of your imagination. Explore a realm where the eerie and the everyday converge, weaving stories that will leave you pondering the mysteries of the unknown.

1

THE NIGHT SHIFT

LET'S JOURNEY THROUGH THE GHOSTLY remnants of a time-honored hospital, where the ancient bricks bear the imprints of forgotten tales. As you explore, the echoes of history resonate through the worn corridors, drawing you into a captivating narrative.

Meet Brandon Rhodes, a twenty-three-year-old thrown into uncertainty as he becomes a security guard at this ancient institution. Determined, he navigates the deserted hallways, finding purpose in his role. Starting part-time, the job fits into his college routine, balancing work and education.

Little does Brandon know, the hospital's hidden history reveals itself during his nightly patrols, adding unexpected complexity to his once-ideal job. The ordinary shadows now hold mysterious secrets, transforming Brandon's view of his role into something intricate.

Meet Brandon Rhodes, a twenty-three-year-old thrown into uncertainty as he becomes a security guard at this ancient institution. Determined, he navigates the deserted hallways, finding purpose in his role. Starting part-time, the job fits into his college routine, balancing work and education.

Little does Brandon know, the hospital's hidden history reveals itself during his nightly patrols, adding unexpected complexity to his once-ideal job. The ordinary shadows now hold mysterious secrets, transforming Brandon's view of his role into something intricate.

Echoes in the Hallways

The aging and worn-out structure radically transformed a year before Brandon started his security job there. The metamorphosis was so profound that it elevated the once dilapidated building into an awe-inspiring five-story marvel, unveiling a storied past that stretched back to the 1900s. The echoes of this architectural rebirth weren't just physical; they permeated the air with an almost tangible sense of revitalization.

What Brandon didn't realize upon assuming his role as a security guard was that the significance of his involvement transcended the routine responsibilities of safeguarding the premises. Unbeknownst to him, he became an unwitting participant in a larger narrative intricately woven into the very essence of the building's newfound grandeur. Like an unseen thread, this narrative connected him to the historical tapestry of the place, revealing layers of stories waiting to be explored and understood. In essence, Brandon found himself not just guarding the physical security of the building but also standing on the threshold of an unfolding tale that intertwined with the rich history and renewed vitality of the architectural masterpiece he now patrolled.

The hospital boasted expansive hallways stretching across every floor, with rooms that seemed to whisper hidden tales. A contemporary elevator on one side promised a swift journey through the building's core. In contrast, a staircase on the opposite end invited a leisurely exploration. This architectural transformation wasn't merely a physical facelift; it was a living narrative woven into the hospital's walls, a story waiting to be uncovered by those courageous enough to explore its depths. As a security guard, Brandon found himself unexpectedly at the heart of this unfolding tale, woven into the very essence of the building.

However, the tranquility of the hospital's new construction was shattered six months post-completion. In a bewildering turn of events, every patient, doctor, and nurse abruptly abandoned the premises, leaving behind a trove of medical tools and supplies. The exodus created a haunting tableau, with half-empty coffee mugs, wheelchairs, and impeccably hung uniforms serving as eerie remnants. The sudden departure remained cloaked in mystery.

Graveyard Shift Anomalies

Before starting his shift, Brandon conversed with the daytime security guard. The guard divulged peculiar occurrences at the hospital during the day, offering Brandon valuable insights into potential incidents he might encounter during his watch. Specifically, there had been reports of furniture rearrangement on the third floor at night. Taking heed of this information, the guard advised Brandon to exercise heightened vigilance in monitoring that particular area.

Brandon undertook his responsibilities during the graveyard shift. He found comfort in the seemingly vacant and tranquil atmosphere enveloping the building. The regularity of navigating hushed corridors, scrutinizing rooms, and safeguarding against potential vandalism or intrusion presented a straightforward routine.

On the second day of his shift, a troubling trend emerged. Doors that he diligently secured required locking again when he circled back. A constant light in a room on the fourth floor grabbed his notice. Despite casually turning it off during his first rounds, Brandon was astonished to see it flicker back on when he came around again.

Curious, Brandon looked into the strange happening, thinking it might be a glitch. Yet, as he approached the flickering light, things turned surprisingly. Footsteps echoed upstairs, and a door squeaked shut on the floor Brandon had just checked. Not discouraged, he went up to the fifth floor to explore, only to see the elevator acting independently, going from floor to floor. Phones kept ringing nonstop, and nurse call lights blinked uncontrollably.

Confronted by this unusual sequence of events, Brandon maintained his composure, attributing the peculiar incidents to potential electrical glitches within the building. Unbeknownst to him, the hospital's mysterious history had intricately woven itself into the fabric of his nightly routine, subtly setting the stage for an unfolding narrative of the inexplicable.

Brandon's Unearthly Vigil

The following day, Brandon did his patrol route. He noticed one of the lights was on in the locked hallway rooms, the same room as last time. Brandon knew it didn't make sense for the light to be on because Brandon had checked it yesterday. Nevertheless, he unlocks the door, turns off the light, and relocks it. As he began to walk away, he heard the light switch on. Brandon slowly peered through the door's frosted glass and saw that the light was on again. He slowly unlocked the door and looked around the room. But there was no one. So, he switched the light off, locked the door, and left. A little nervous, he still brushed it off and returned to the hallway for the remainder of the night.

On the fourth night of his shift, Brandon decided to alter his routine, initiating his patrol on the fifth floor and descending via the elevator. As he ascended, he discerned faint laughter and conversation echoing in the background. The voices grew louder in tandem with the elevator's ascent, reaching their peak as soon as he got to the top floor. Abruptly, all sounds ceased, but the entire fifth floor illuminated as if activated by an unseen force, with the patient rooms bathed in light and phones ringing loudly. Astonished by this eerie turn of events, Brandon, convinced he had heard voices, was determined to uncover the source. Vigilantly searching for an intruder, he found no one in sight.

The fifth night unfolded like the preceding ones, enveloped in an eerie hush. Brandon, situated on the fourth floor, diligently secured all the doors along the corridor. In the dim glow, he observed the room with the frosted glass door slightly ajar once again. Upon closer inspection, everything appeared ordinary until an unmistakable silhouette of a person traversed past him and out the door. Brandon, unequivocal in his account, vividly described it as a "clear as day" shadow of a person. In response, adrenaline surged through him, propelling him to chase after the mysterious figure. However, as he pursued, it inexplicably vanished, triggering an overwhelming sense of disbelief and apprehension encapsulated by a resounding "Screw this shit!" feeling. Despite cherishing his time at the hospital, Brandon became increasingly unsettled by these unexplained phenomena.

Adding to the tension, more security guards working different shifts shared unsettling stories similar to Brandon's experiences. They spoke of recurring encounters, specifically seeing shadowy figures resembling nuns wandering through the patient rooms on the third floor. Despite these collective and eerie stories, a clear explanation for the strange happenings in the abandoned hospital remained elusive. The accounts from the security guards contributed to an atmosphere of mystery and unease surrounding the deserted facility.

Chased by Shadows

It seems our unsuspecting security guard, Brandon, walked right into the heart of a ghostly tale. The once-dilapidated hospital, reborn into a grand marvel, held more than just echoes of its past. It clutched a bizarre narrative that unfolded with every creaking door and flickering light.

As Brandon delved deeper into his nightly routine, the hospital's secrets unfurled like a sinister tapestry. Doors locked and unlocked themselves, lights played eerie games, and the fifth floor echoed with spectral laughter. But it wasn't just Brandon witnessing this macabre dance; other guards spoke of shadowy figures, nuns in the night, weaving their unsettling stories.

Our brave security guard, determined to

unravel the mystery, chased shadows that slipped through his grasp. The once tranquil halls echoed whispers of a history that refused to rest in peace. Phones rang relentlessly, doors opened of their own accord, and the abandoned hospital became a stage for the unexplained.

Yet, despite the shared accounts and the palpable unease hanging in the air, the true nature of these spectral occurrences remained elusive. Now a haunted monument to its past, the hospital stood as a testament to the inexplicable forces within its walls.

And so, dear viewers, the story of Brandon and the haunted hospital leaves us with more questions than answers. Some tales are destined to remain shrouded in the shadows, echoing their mysteries through the haunted corridors of the unknown.

2

ENIGMA IN LOUISIANA

LET'S DIVE INTO THE MURKY DEPTHS of southern Louisiana, where tragedy and mystery intertwine in a swampy graveyard of forgotten souls. It was the 1950s when the bayou whispered secrets, and the night held more than just shadows. A plane bearing the destiny of over 200 lives crashed into the unforgiving swamplands below. Rescue attempts proved fruitless, thwarted by the swamp's ravenous inhabitants and the otherworldly presence clinging to the air like moss on a haunted cypress.

But the story veers into the winding paths monitored by Officer Nialle Delgado, a skeptic confronting the supernatural. Little did he realize that the swamp's secrets weren't confined to the wreckage but lingered on, poised to surface beneath the cover of night.

Join in as we unfold the eerie tale I call Enigma

in Louisiana, where the boundary between the living and the lost becomes indistinct. The swamp resounds with the haunting cries of the departed. Get your popcorn, dim the lights, and prepare for a journey into the depths of darkness.

Swamp Legends

During the 1950s, in the remote expanse of southern Louisiana, an enigmatic tragedy unfolded as a plane carrying a staggering number of over 200 individuals plunged mysteriously into the murky swamplands below. The crash hit hard, making it challenging for the rescue teams to get all the bodies back. To make matters worse, hungry swamp alligators grabbed whatever was left before the recovery crews could enter.

Back then, with little fancy tech around and hardly any clues left from the big crash, the folks in charge sadly couldn't figure out what went down on that hot summer night. Since they couldn't nail down the facts, the folks who cared about the people involved put up a sad statue by the swamp. It rests by the roadside, a lasting reminder of the unfortunate event in the remote areas of Louisiana.

After the turbulent event, time has spun stories of ghosts and apparitions in the lonely swamp where a plane crashed. Despite the stories, the memorial structure is the only enduring reminder of the tragedy. The swamp has erased all signs of the catastrophic plane crash, letting nature thrive again in areas once marked by charred devastation.

As the years passed, a profound hesitation took root, particularly among the older generation, who still recall the unsettling incident vividly. This reluctance prevents them from venturing down the road near the mysterious swamp, especially after dark. Visitors share chilling experiences, from eerie cries to ghostly figures wandering around the tragedy site. These haunting events notably heighten on the anniversary, adding an extra layer of spookiness to the already unsettling atmosphere of this ghostly place.

Midnight Whispers

Upon joining the Louisiana Police Force after moving from California, Nialle Delgado initially firmly held skepticism toward anything paranormal. A subtle amusement crossed his face as he heard local stories about ghosts in the swamp. Assigned to an area with frequent traffic violations, the locale became a prime spot for catching speeders and intoxicated drivers, especially on busy weekends. Tucked away on a quiet back road, the region had gained a reputation as a route where reckless drivers thought they could operate without consequences.

While bonding with fellow officers, Officer Delgado received cautionary advice. His colleagues earnestly shared warnings about the ghostly legends surrounding the swamp. Undeterred, he brushed off their words with a hearty laugh, chalking up the tales to a collective effort to test his composure and stake a claim on his preferred posting within the force.

Assigned consistently to his designated post, Officer Delgado spent his days apprehending a steady stream of speeding drivers. At times, the traffic was so relentless that he remained stationed in front of the memorial monument for his entire shift. After a few days of this dedicated routine, the Chief approached Officer Delgado with a specific request—to take charge of the night shift. The Chief's goal was to reduce the alarming number of DUI-related fatalities on that particular stretch of road. Intrigued by the opportunity and valuing the solitude promised by the overnight hours, Officer Delgado readily agreed to the Chief's directive.

Bizarre Encounter

As Officer Delgado commenced his shift, he maneuvered his vehicle into the customary position, meticulously arranging his radar setup. The hour hadn't seen the rowdy departure of bar patrons yet, leaving the road strangely calm. The only audible sounds were the croaking frogs in the swamp behind him. Immersed in catching up on paperwork, his fingers danced across the keyboard when a subtle thump echoed beyond the walls of his patrol car.

Paused by the sound, Officer Delgado's sharp senses tuned in to the surroundings. The swamp's nighttime chorus resumed, and with no repeat of the disturbance after a few minutes, he went back to his administrative tasks, thinking the initial thump was probably just a local alligator going about its routine movements. Yet, the calm was short-lived. A follow-up scratching emerged, starting on the car's passenger side and moving methodically toward the back before suddenly stopping. This injected an unexpected sense of suspense into the previously peaceful night.

Aware of the various creatures in the area, Officer Delgado, dressed in tactical gear and armed, carefully opened the car door. Before stepping out, he checked beneath the vehicle thoroughly, watchful for any potential threats hiding in the shadows. Systematically, he walked around the car, using his flashlight to pierce the darkness and light up the surroundings, including the mysterious stretch of the swamp. The immediate area showed no apparent signs of disturbance.

Bending down, Officer Delgado examined the strange marks on the side of his patrol car, his fingers following the outlines of what seemed to be ash or dust. Two long streaks ran down to the bumper, stopping mysteriously. During his investigation, an unexpected breeze rushed through the swamp, sending a shiver down his spine. Brushing off the uneasy feeling with a determined laugh, he returned to his vehicle's safety, resuming his duties with unwavering professionalism.

Carrying out his usual routine the next night,

Officer Delgado was deeply engrossed in the familiar rhythm of his duties. Around two hours into his watch, the mysterious noise returned, this time echoing with heightened intensity. Quickly stepping out of the patrol car, he scanned the surroundings, only to find the lively antics of leaping frogs. His investigative instincts kicked in, prompting him to circle the vehicle and reveal an expanded layer of dark soot on the passenger side.

Inhaling deeply, Officer Delgado caught a strong whiff of fuel and burning, a sharp sting reaching his nostrils. Scanning the surroundings, he entertained the idea that something might be on fire. Still, the darkness revealed no signs of an impending blaze. For a moment, he thought about the eerie stories describing the scent of the plane's burning fuel on that fateful night. However, he quickly laughed off such thoughts, playfully scolding himself for entertaining ideas that ventured into the supernatural realm.

Eerie Spectacle

On his last night patrolling the evening shift, Officer Delgado settled into his patrol car, watching the road for potential speeders. Much like the previous evenings, a troubling scratching noise once again pierced the ambient tranquility as the night unfolded. Reacting quickly, he leaped out of the vehicle, his call echoing into the night air. An eerie silence ensued, abruptly interrupted by the sinister scent of burning fuel pervading the surroundings. Bending down to inspect the car's surface, Officer Delgado's eyes widened as he discovered a tiny handprint etched onto the vehicle this time.

Suddenly standing, a shiver raced down his spine, making the hair on the back of his neck stand on end. The frogs, once lively inhabitants of the swamp, fell silent, replaced by an unsettling chorus of what sounded like distant cries. The mournful wails grew louder, becoming a crescendo akin to a bustling stadium crowd. Panic took hold as Officer Delgado, rooted in place, anxiously surveyed the mysterious scene unfolding around him, wrestling with an unspoken fear that surpassed the confines of rational explanation.

In the swamp, he observed hundreds of glowing orbs that looked like eyes blinking in his direction. With the persistent cries, the scent of jet fuel, and the eerie glow of those eyes, Officer Delgado reached his limit. He sped away, leaving nothing but the dust from his tires. Even now, people claim to hear the cries for help from the 200 lost souls who perished there many years ago.

Enigma in Louisiana

And so, as the clock ticks and shadows dance, we find Officer Nialle Delgado thrust into the heart of a supernatural symphony. The lonely swamp, once the silent witness to a tragic demise, unveils its ghostly secrets with each passing night.

Once a skeptic in a sea of spectral tales, Officer

Delgado grapples with the inexplicable. The scratching, the scent of burning fuel, and the tiny handprint etched into the metal of his patrol car — all whispers from the other side, demanding to be heard. The swamp, now a stage for ethereal apparitions, weaves a chilling tale that echoes through time.

As he peels away, leaving behind the haunting cries and glowing eyes, Officer Delgado carries an indelible mark — a testament to the thin veil separating the living from the beyond. Once a mere stretch of pavement, the road transforms into a gateway where the departed beckon to the living.

In the stillness of the Louisiana night, the whispers persist. The tragic souls, forever lost in the murky depths, reach out to the living, their voices woven into the fabric of the haunted swamp. And so, the legend endures — a spectral reminder of the enigmatic tragedy that forever binds the living and the dead in the heart of the mysterious, ghostly place known as the Enigma in Louisiana.

3

THE DORMITORY OF SECRETS

STEP INTO THE WORLD OF ACADEMIA, where the echoes of history linger in the hallways, undisturbed by the constant buzz of fluorescent lights. This is a story of dormitory secrets, where the old walls bear the weight of more than just the passage of time.

In a small Ohio town, the University's dorms, built in the 1960s, became witnesses to a history marked by the supernatural. A guardian of order, Officer Mitch Bailey discovered himself in a nightmare within those echoing corridors. But be warned, this isn't merely a ghost tale; it's a journey into the shadows where the paranormal meets the hidden secrets embedded in the very foundation of the University.

Dormitory of Secrets

The University's dormitories, constructed in the 1960s, exhibited signs of aging, particularly the initial three levels of the women's dorms, which had remained unchanged since their inception. The outdated interior design, characterized by orange shag carpets, unmistakably conveyed the passage of time. Given the college's pivotal role in the small Ohio town, contributing significantly to its annual income, the administrators recognized the need to enhance the University's appeal. To make the university more attractive to a broader range of students and improve its overall appeal, the administrators decided to give the dorms a complete makeover with a modern look.

While the renovations were happening, it was discovered that some college students were misusing the space for unauthorized parties when resident advisors weren't around, causing incidents of vandalism. Consequently, the University opted to bolster security by engaging off-duty police officers from the local area seeking additional employment.

Athletic Dreams

Officer Mitch Bailey found the job to be a perfect fit as he was finishing up his education, contributing to the department, and looking to earn some extra income. The routine remained generally tranquil, with occasional bursts of liveliness occurring when the local bars emptied. On typical nights, Officer Bailey's main task was patrolling the dormitory hallways.

During a routine patrol of the dormitories, he stumbled upon interesting historical artifacts that unveiled the true intent behind the engineers' design. The building was initially meant to be the home for the State Championship-winning girls' softball team. The blueprints and historical documents he unearthed vividly illustrated the college's ambitious vision to foster athletic excellence. However, as the college's academic programs thrived and the student body grew, the demand for housing surpassed the existing facilities. As a result, additional dormitories were built to accommodate the expanding campus community.

Officer Bailey's deep connection to the world of sports, forged through years of playing ball passionately and actively participating in the Police Department's recreational league, brought a unique perspective to his role. His history of dedication to athletic pursuits and community engagement added a distinctive dimension to the unfolding story of the structures that once harbored championship aspirations for a spirited softball team.

Playmate

During one of Officer Bailey's nightly patrols through the dormitory corridors, he stumbled upon a box brimming with a trove of old trophies and photographs chronicling the achievements of bygone teams. As he sifted through the contents, memories of his college baseball days came rushing back. At the bottom of the box, he discovered an old softball, a relic from the dorm's rich history. Intrigued, Bailey decided to pick it up, cradling the time-worn ball as he continued his leisurely stroll through the different floors of the dormitory.

As Officer Bailey made his way through the second floor, he encountered an unexpected obstacle—a broom sprawled across the floor. Unfortunately, the softball he carried slipped from his grip and started rolling playfully down the hallway. Attempting to stop its course, Bailey could only watch as it swiftly rolled into an empty room. Bailey laughed at his clumsiness, but amusement didn't last long as the hallway lights flickered. Puzzled, he glanced down and found the same softball at his feet. Intrigued and slightly puzzled, Officer Bailey picked up the ball, checking to ensure it was the same. Looking around the hallway and the room it had rolled into, Bailey found himself alone, thinking about the strange sequence of events.

Considering the possibility of a prank, Officer Bailey chuckled and playfully rolled the ball down the hallway. To his surprise, the ball suddenly stopped as if someone had grabbed it out of thin air, defying the laws of physics. Intrigued but maintaining a healthy dose of skepticism, Bailey stepped back, squinting to examine the strange occurrence. Seeing the ball levitate before him, he dismissed any supernatural thoughts with a sarcastic remark, saying, "Ohhh, big scary ghost," followed by laughter. Convinced that it was an elaborate practical joke, Bailey stuck to his belief that someone was orchestrating a playful trick.

Dean's Dark Secret

His laughter dwindled into wary silence as the lights urgently flickered. Doors in the vicinity started to swing wildly, generating a tumultuous symphony of slamming and reopening, resonating with loud bangs. Shifting his focus back to the mysteriously floating ball, Officer Bailey witnessed it accelerating through the air, seemingly heading straight for his head. Reacting quickly, he skillfully dodged to the right, narrowly avoiding the flying object. The ball collided with the wall behind him, exerting considerable force and leaving a conspicuous dent.

Retreating cautiously, Officer Bailey experienced a brisk wind sweeping through the hallway, unsettling dust and rustling old papers. A surge of indescribable anger turned into a sense of dread as he witnessed unexplained events unfolding. Suddenly, the tempest stopped, and the settled dust gracefully fell to the floor. A disconcerting tapping sound drew his attention to the doorframe.

With trembling hands, Bailey cautiously retraced his steps to the mysterious room. Inside, there was movement but no corresponding shadow. Slowly turning toward the open doorway, he was confronted with a haunting sight – a ghostly apparition of a young girl hanging from the rafters. Wearing her softball uniform, she held her mitt with an eerie stillness. Backing away with increasing unease, Bailey accidentally stepped on a creaky floor beam. The ghostly figure, hanging from the rafters, suddenly turned her head toward Bailey, her ethereal face expressing anger.

In a moment of panic, Officer Bailey quickly left his keys behind, rushed down the stairs, and fled the building. That night, from the safety of his home, he dug into the dormitory's unsettling history. His investigation unveiled a chilling narrative: the coach dismissed a softball player from the team only a year before the dorm reassignments. Sadly, upon her return to the dorms, she took her own life by hanging herself in one of the hallways.

The disturbing discoveries didn't stop there; during Bailey's investigation, reports of malevolent hauntings in that housing wing emerged. Students shared stories of doors slamming, mirrors breaking, and unsettling screams piercing the quiet night, adding to the eerie history that now clung to those once calm and safe dormitories.

Officer Bailey quickly informed the University Dean about the strange events, expecting a surprised or concerned reaction. Oddly, the Dean showed no such response, almost unaffected by the revelation. A year later, Bailey discovered a surprising change: instead of assigning residents to that floor, the university had turned it into a lounge for academics and socializing. The decision implied a purposeful avoidance of the supernatural occurrences that had plagued the area.

Contemplating the various supernatural incidents, Officer Bailey somberly vowed never to revisit that haunted place. He believed it was better left untouched, serving as a chilling reminder of the unexplainable forces that had made their home within its walls.

Shadows and Concealed Secrets

Officer Mitch Bailey found himself in a nightmarish tale within the university halls. It was a story of restless spirits, a mistreated softball player, and a dormitory marked by tragedy. The winds of the supernatural swept through the aging walls, revealing a past steeped in sorrow and regret.

But here's the twist in this eerie tale – it wasn't just about ghostly apparitions and slamming doors. No, it was the Dean, playing it cool in the face of the supernatural, casually turning a haunted floor into a lounge as if it were just another day.

Some secrets run deep, my friends and not even a ghostly wail can bring them to light.

So, wise in his fear, Officer Bailey decided that some things are better left alone. The once haunted floor, now a calm lounge for books and chats, conceals the echoes of a troubled past. With a solemn promise, Officer Bailey left that past behind, swirling in the shadows of the unexplainable.

As the pages turn, remember, dear listeners, some stories are best shared in whispers, and some places are meant for the ghosts. Until next time, keep those doors locked and your eyes wide open – you never know what might lurk in the shadows of your seemingly quiet dormitory.

4
CHAPEL'S HAUNTING

IN THE QUIET WORLD of Officer Blake Munoz, a seemingly routine patrol takes a chilling turn. As he navigates the moonlit security corridors, shadows whisper of something more than the ordinary. In the heart of a church, Officer Munoz becomes a patrol supervisor with a front-row seat to a collision of the mundane and the unexplainable. Lights flicker, doors creak, and an unsettling history surfaces to cast its ominous veil over the night. Join Officer Munoz on an uncharted journey where reality blurs and the supernatural dances with the living. This is more than a routine patrol; it's a walk through the unexplained.

So, close your doors, lower the lights, and step into a world where the ordinary unravels, and something sinister lingers just beyond. Officer Blake Munoz faces a haunting reality in the enigmatic mysteries that grip the haunted halls of the church.

Phantom Melody

Officer Blake Munoz served as the patrol supervisor for a prominent security firm, overseeing various routes, including safeguarding a substantial complex comprising a sizable church, private daycare, and kindergarten. His official responsibilities extended to conducting comprehensive checks and implementing security measures for the entire facility between 3 a.m. and 4 a.m. Due to reports of doors being left ajar in the morning, Officer Munoz received explicit instructions from the church to diligently verify and secure all access points, thereby mitigating the risk of unauthorized entry and ensuring the safety of the premises.

During Officer Munoz's initial night on duty, he diligently patrolled the assigned church premises, which emanated an unsettling atmosphere that left him feeling uneasy. The building, wrapped in an eerie quiet, heightened his senses as the only audible sound was the resonating echo of his boots traversing the lengthy corridor housing the kindergarten classrooms. Methodically, Officer Munoz conducted a thorough inspection, ensuring the security of each classroom. Upon his return, he was surprised to observe a solitary balloon drifting down the center of the hallway, an unexpected and perplexing occurrence. Startled by the balloon's seemingly random appearance, Officer Munoz promptly retrieved and decommissioned it, addressing the anomaly with swift and decisive action.

On the subsequent evening, Officer Munoz arrived at the church and skillfully parked near the pastor's office. Evidently, the pastor was burning the midnight oil, as indicated by the illumination from his workspace. During his rounds, Officer Munoz directed his attention to the pastor's office. Upon discreetly peering inside, he discerned the pastor's absence. Still, he noted an illuminated lighthouse-shaped lamp on a table, casting its glow towards a substantial window. Swiftly taking charge of the situation, Officer Munoz extinguished the light, meticulously inspected the office, secured all access points, and proceeded with his patrol duties. As Officer Munoz concluded his night shift and prepared to depart in his vehicle, he observed that the light in the pastor's office had been reignited. Opting not to intervene further, he left it undisturbed and returned home.

During the ensuing weekend, the church organized a bustling bake sale, transforming its kitchen into a confectionery haven replete with an array of delectable treats—plates adorned with cookies, cakes, brownies, and more. A considerate staff member thoughtfully left a note extending an open invitation to security personnel to indulge in the tempting assortment of kitchen snacks. Responding to the gesture, Officer Munoz entered the kitchen with the intent of tidying up the culinary display. Amidst the attractive spread, he keenly observed a precise count of twelve chocolate chip cookies resting on the counter, adding a specific detail to the delectable tableau before him.

Upon completing the meticulous cleanup of the kitchen, Officer Munoz discerned a conspicuous absence of cookies when he returned to the counter to retrieve the cookie plate. What initially presented as a bountiful collection had diminished significantly, leaving only three cookies in its wake. Perplexingly, there was no one else within the confines of the building who could have been accountable for the diminution of the delectable treats. The unexpected discrepancy raised questions, casting a shroud of intrigue over the seemingly deserted premises.

Officer Munoz routinely grappled with a perplexing phenomenon involving doors that, despite being securely closed and locked, exhibited an uncanny tendency to open and unlock autonomously, all transpiring in the eerie absence of any other individuals. Such unexplainable occurrences were not exclusive to Officer Munoz, as other officers assigned to this church reported encountering similarly mystifying incidents. Notably, the officer who assumed Officer Munoz's duties for a single night abruptly resigned the next day, citing an undisclosed unsettling experience.

During an investigation within the chapel, Officer Munoz confronted another enigma when the pipe organ, devoid of any human presence, commenced playing a melody on its own. This unanticipated orchestration added yet another layer of inexplicable occurrences to the already mysterious atmosphere surrounding the church.

Faced with a series of inexplicable security incidents, Officer Munoz sought insight into the church's history from a knowledgeable staff member. The staff member elucidated that, dating back to the early 1900s, the tower served as a modest schoolhouse. Tragically, a devastating fire engulfed the school at some point, claiming the lives of several children who were trapped within its confines. The historical narrative provided a haunting backdrop to the peculiar events Officer Munoz and his colleagues were experiencing. Astonishingly, after only a brief week of overseeing the church's security, Officer Munoz formally requested the removal of the church from his patrol route, undoubtedly influenced by the chilling history that now imbued the place with an unsettling aura.

Chilly Moonlit

Officer Munoz stumbled into something weird that gives you the creeps, like a chilly wind on a moonlit night. He was used to odd things, patrolling a church that held secrets darker than its shadows. Doors opened by themselves, ghostly tunes from a long-gone organ, and a history filled with sorrow – the stuff of nightmares.

It wasn't just Munoz; his colleagues faced the

unknown, too. One poor soul, covering for Munoz one night, ran away faster than you can say "haunted." And those disappearing cookies added a sweet twist to the spooky. Twelve became three, blamed on the ghostly whispers of departed kids.

As Munoz dug into the church's past, he found a tragic tale. The place was once a schoolhouse turned inferno, taking innocent children with it. Their echoes lingered in every creak and flicker of light. In a week, Munoz had enough of the eerie. The ghosts of the past had him in their icy grip, and he wanted out. He said his goodbyes to the haunted chapel, asking for a different gig.

So, the church stood, silent witness to a history filled with sadness, Munoz's footsteps fading into the night—a warning for those who tread where the line between the living and the dead blurs.

5

PHOTOGRAPHIC MALEVOLENCE

GATHER AROUND AS WE UNCOVER, a tale straddling the line between the known and the mysterious. In the dim world of crime, there's a photographer with a steady gaze, capturing shadows on the edges of reality.

Meet Tara Gibbs, a seasoned figure behind the lens. She's witnessed chilling crime scenes, unraveling dark mysteries for ten years. But in her pursuit of the unseen, Gibbs stumbles upon a case that blurs the lines between the tangible and the supernatural.

Brace yourselves for a journey into the unknown. Amidst a career marked by violent scenes, Gibbs is caught in a web of supernatural encounters. The ordinary and the otherworldly intertwine, placing our intrepid Crime Scene Photographer at the crossroads of reality and the unexplained.

As we explore this spectral saga, remember that not all mysteries are apparent. Sometimes, the most bizarre tales unfold in the quiet spaces between heartbeats, where unseen shadows reveal a truth beyond the logic of the living.

Get ready for a plunge into the cryptic as we reveal the haunting chronicles of Tara Gibbs and the enigma that lurks in the shadows of her unyielding lens.

Ethereal Backdrop

For a decade, Tara Gibbs had been the unwavering stalwart behind the lens of her camera, capturing the chilling tapestry of crime scenes that unfolded in the local shadows. Her role as the Crime Scene Photographer had endowed her with an unyielding gaze that confronted the darkest corners of humanity. While the macabre nature of her work repelled many, it became a peculiar refuge for Gibbs. Through the unblinking eye of her camera, she found solace, an avenue to unveil the obscure traces of malevolence that eluded the naked eye.

In the realm of death and misfortune, Gibbs had traversed a gruesome spectrum, from the haunting aftermath of fatal accidents to the eerie silence of hospital malpractice. No calamity was foreign to her lens – plane crashes, car wrecks, and the grotesque tableau of violent demises. The crimson tapestry of blood and gore had woven itself into the fabric of her professional existence. Colleagues, in vain attempts to unsettle her, sought to stir unease. Still, Gibbs stood unshaken, a bastion of composure in the face of the macabre.

On a somber evening, the piercing ring of Gibbs' phone heralded a grim assignment: a double homicide. The urgency in the caller's voice emphasized the critical need for her immediate presence at the crime scene. The victims, a mother and child, cast a pall of sorrow over the investigation, demanding meticulous documentation. At the same time, their lifeless forms still lay undisturbed. The investigators, acutely aware of the fleeting nature of crucial evidence, entrusted Gibbs with the task of preserving the crime scene's integrity through her lens.

The gravity of the situation bore down on Gibbs, yet she remained resolute. While the cold efficiency of capturing images did not faze her, the subject matter was a bitter pill to swallow. Photographing the lifeless remains felt like navigating an emotionally treacherous terrain, mainly when innocent children were involved. The clash between the professional necessity for unerring documentation and the emotional toll of such scenes lingered as a disconcerting undercurrent, casting a shadow over Gibbs' otherwise composed demeanor.

Swiftly arriving at the weathered expanse of an old warehouse apartment building, Gibbs ascended to the pinnacle, where the family had meticulously refurbished their living space. The apartment, adorned with floor-to-ceiling windows in the living room, served as the haunting backdrop for her latest assignment. With efficient precision, she methodically captured images of the lifeless forms and the forensic landscape that surrounded them.

Yet, the task needed to be completed. As the coroners undertook their solemn duty to clear the bodies, Gibbs remained tethered to the crime scene, poised to extract additional layers of visual evidence. Completing the initial set of photographs, she emerged into the outside world, craving the solace of fresh air and the comforting embrace of a cup of coffee. However, an unsettling sensation crept over her as she descended the service stairs. An inexplicable discomfort lingered an ethereal presence that seemed to accompany her steps. Shrugging off the disquiet, Gibbs attributed it to the inherent unease of capturing the stillness of a deceased child through the lens of her camera.

However, an elusive weight clung to her chest, an indescribable sensation that defied release. Emotions surged within her, and a tumultuous cascade gripped her with an unusual ferocity. A tempest of fury raged within Gibbs, a stark departure from the composed detachment cultivated over a decade of capturing the macabre through her lens. Puzzlingly, the source of this intense upheaval remained obscured, an enigma that left Gibbs grappling with unprecedented turmoil.

Stepping into the embrace of the outside world, the oppressive emotion lifted, dissipating like morning mist in the presence of sunlight. In the open air, Gibbs found a respite, a temporary reprieve from the emotional maelstrom that had seized her. Braced against the elements, she patiently awaited the moment to reenter the confines of the crime scene, determined to resume her duty and confront the unresolved unease that lingered within.

A Strange Presence

After the coroner had meticulously relocated the lifeless forms, Gibbs ascended the stairs to commence the second phase of her photographic documentation. Her usual protocol involved requesting the staff's evacuation of the room to ensure no detail escaped her lens. Yet, within the frigid confines of the apartment, as she relentlessly captured images of blood-stained floors, an unsettling emotion resurfaced, sending a shiver down her spine. The air seemed charged with an intangible force, causing the fine hairs on her neck to stand on end.

Each snap of the camera acted as a dissonant chord, amplifying the intensity of the inexplicable feelings until Gibbs, momentarily overwhelmed, halted to draw a fortifying breath. Concerned officers checked on her well-being, attempting to lighten the mood with jests about spectral entities haunting her. However, humor found no purchase in Gibbs' disconcerted state. She hastened to conclude the task, completing the final photographs with urgency before swiftly retreating from the haunting milieu within. Just as before, the oppressive sensation relinquished its hold the moment she crossed the threshold into the open air beyond the front door.

In the hushed confines of the station, Gibbs diligently printed the photographic chronicle of the crime scene. Fatigue hung heavy in the air, a tangible reminder of the arduous task. Confronted with a daunting array of several hundred images, she methodically categorized them into distinct piles, each representing a fragment of the enigma she sought to unravel. Exhaustion intermingled with determination as she delved into the visual narrative, forging a gritty resolve.

Amidst the fatigue-laden review, Gibbs found herself clutching a bundle of photographs, only to be confronted by a chilling tableau—a window adorned with a bloody handprint. Disbelief etched across her features, she instinctively flicked on the harsh fluorescence of the conference room light, where the gravity of the images could be dissected with greater clarity. The pictures sprawled across the table, a mosaic of macabre details demanding her attention.

A wave of melancholy washed over Gibbs as her hand instinctively sought solace over her chest. The emotional undercurrents of the crime scene, once suppressed, now surged to the forefront, leaving her grappling with a profound sense of sadness. In that moment, the images before her ceased to be mere documentation; they became fragments of a tragedy that transcended the confines of the photograph, echoing within the recesses of Gibbs' weary psyche.

In each photograph capturing the window, an eerie repetition unfolded — a mother cradling her child, an unsettling presence lurking just behind Gibbs in the reflective glass. While the lens immortalized a scene of sorrow, the countenance of the victim betrayed not grief but a seething rage. The poignant fusion of emotions resonated through the images, casting a haunting tableau where, with each burst of light, the woman's face contorted in a silent scream of unbridled anger reverberating across the confines of the photograph. The juxtaposition of maternal tenderness and furious despair painted a disquieting portrait, leaving Gibbs entrapped in a visual narrative transcending the boundaries of mere documentation.

Within the confines of that apartment, a specter of violence lingered, its echoes reverberating through the lens of Gibbs's camera. The residual presence of enraged spirits manifested in the very fabric of her photographs an ethereal testament to the lingering anger that pervaded the crime scene. Despite her seasoned expertise, Gibbs grappled with an unprecedented unease, a disquieting connection to the spectral remnants that infused her visual documentation.

Confronted with the palpable intensity of the haunted imagery, Gibbs carried the weight of the ethereal encounters to her Chief. Acknowledging the need for another investigator to navigate the unsettling aftermath, she relinquished the case, a rare concession in her otherwise unyielding resolve. The enigma surrounding this crime scene, fraught with malevolent apparitions and unexplained emotions, persisted as an unsolvable mystery in Gibbs's repertoire. A chapter in her storied career marked by an inexplicable connection to the supernatural, destined to remain eternally shrouded in the shadows of the unexplained.

Lingering Shadows

As we plunge deeper into the twisted tapestry of Tara Gibbs' career, we find ourselves entangled in the spectral strands of the macabre. Like snapshots of a nightmare, the photographs reveal a darkness that transcends the boundaries of mere mortal understanding. Our intrepid Crime Scene Photographer, once an unyielding stalwart behind the lens, now stands at the precipice of a mystery that defies resolution.

In the silent corridors of that haunted apartment, where bloodstains spoke of tragedy, Gibbs unwittingly captured more than just the aftermath of violence. The anguished spirits, restless and enraged, left their ethereal imprints on her photographs, a chilling testament to the lingering anger that clung to the crime scene like a vengeful specter.

As our tale unfurls, seasoned and unshaken Gibbs confronts an unprecedented unease. The visual narrative she painstakingly uncovered reveals a dance between maternal tenderness and furious despair, a disquieting portrait transcending the boundaries of a mere crime scene. The images, infused with an otherworldly intensity, become more than documentation; they become fragments of a tragedy etched into the fabric of Gibbs' weary psyche.

Faced with the palpable presence of the supernatural, our relentless protagonist makes an unusual concession. She relinquishes the case, acknowledging the need for another investigator to navigate the unsettling aftermath. The enigma surrounding this crime scene, fraught with malevolent apparitions and unexplained emotions, remains an unsolvable mystery in Gibbs' storied career.

And so, dear listeners, we bid adieu to Tara Gibbs. This unyielding lens dared to capture the unseen, the unexplained. A chapter marked by an inexplicable connection to the supernatural, destined to remain eternally shrouded in the shadows of the unexplained. As the cryptic echoes of this spectral encounter linger, we are left to ponder the chilling question: what unseen presences await in the shadows of our own reality?

6

NIGHTMARE PATROL

STEP INTO THE MYSTERIOUS TOWN OF SALEM, Massachusetts, renowned for its captivating history, associations with witchcraft, and an air of eerie uncertainty. Follow Officer Tony Hansen through his usual nights in Salem, which veer unexpectedly into darkness. Accompany us as we navigate the supernatural aspects woven into his nightly patrols, obscuring the distinction between what is reality and the paranormal. Brace yourself for a peculiar odyssey as Officer Hansen confronts the unexplained and grapples with the decision to adhere to reason or embrace the unsettling mysteries concealed in the shadows. Welcome to a chapter marked by unexplainable occurrences and the disquieting choice between rationality and the supernatural on the dimly illuminated streets of Salem.

Haunted Outskirts

In Salem, Massachusetts, Tony Hansen's upbringing immersed him in a world of ghost stories, the town's historical backdrop and association with witchcraft creating a distinct atmosphere. Unbeknownst to him, these narratives would play a significant role in shaping his future. As he grew older, Tony chose to pursue a career as a Police Officer, following in the footsteps of those who maintained order in the historic city. Salem's captivating history, interwoven with supernatural tales, seamlessly became a part of his daily existence.

When Officer Hansen started as a rookie cop, his coworkers enjoyed telling him spooky stories. It was a way of bonding and sharing experiences. The tales served as a form of initiation, a lighthearted tradition, before he embarked on solo patrols through the dimly lit streets of Salem.

Despite the entertaining narratives, Officer Hansen quickly realized that the reality of the night held a different tone. As he patrolled around the quiet and dark parts of the old city, the spooky feeling from the stories didn't happen. The spectral presence hinted at in the tales remained elusive, leaving Officer Hansen to conclude that, for him, the ghostly narratives were mere figments of imagination and not a tangible part of his nocturnal patrols. The once foreboding tales became nothing more than folklore echoing through the stillness of the Salem nights.

However, a significant shift occurred when Officer Hansen assumed the responsibility of patrolling the city's outskirts. The community had been abuzz with rumors of ritual sacrifices and ghostly apparitions a decade prior, sparking concern among the residents. Despite the widespread talk, Officer Hansen had dismissed these stories as pure fiction. Undeterred, he proceeded with his routine night shift, directing his attention toward the city's western outskirts. The darkness was profound, with only the moon providing a feeble glow, casting eerie shadows that seemed to animate, intensifying the overall sense of unease.

Eerie Resonance

Officer Hansen sat in a quiet part of the neighborhood, surrounded by the deep silence of the night. At first, Officer Hansen did his usual paperwork, but things turned unsettling. Weird sounds echoed near his parked patrol car, breaking the usual calm. Even though he tried to stay calm, Officer Hansen couldn't shake off the uneasy feeling creeping into his mind.

Faced with strange sounds, Officer Hansen turned on his patrol car's lights to light up the area. He squinted into the darkness, carefully looking around to determine where the unsettling noise was coming from. However, to his confusion, there was no discernible anomaly. To calm himself down, Officer Hansen convinced himself that the alarming noises were probably caused by a wild animal, which isn't unusual during quiet nights.

Officer Hansen returned to work, trying to make the night normal again. But this calmness didn't last. The unusual sounds returned, louder and faster, defying the typical behavior of nocturnal animals. Officer Hansen became more alert, realizing something strange was happening in the darkness. The seemingly routine task of completing paperwork had suddenly thrust Officer Hansen into an unusual situation, disrupting the usual flow of his nightly patrol and leaving him uncertain about what mysterious events might unfold next.

Officer Hansen exited his patrol vehicle to inspect for damage and identify the person or creature behind the disturbance. In the quiet night, he shouted out, anticipating a reply. Still, only silence echoed, with no footprints near his car.

Feeling confused but not giving up, Officer Hansen returned to his car, thinking whatever caused the disturbance must have disappeared. As he reached for the door, though, it slammed shut, surprising him. Quick to react, he pulled out his weapon and shone his flashlight inside, ready to confront anyone inside. But to his surprise, the car was empty.

Despite the lingering unease, Officer Hansen disregarded the peculiar feeling, chalking it up to the possibility of an unexplained event. Grappling with the uncertainty, he reasoned that there might be a rational explanation for what occurred. Nevertheless, a subtle discomfort persisted throughout the rest of his shift.

Shadowy Watch

The following night, Officer Hansen conducted his regular patrol of the town. Initially, a sense of tranquility permeated the neighborhood, creating a peaceful atmosphere. But things took a turn when a sudden call reported a possible home invasion. A couple had spotted someone casually walking through their backyard. Officer Hansen quickly responded, eager to check out what was happening and ensure the community was safe and secure.

Upon responding promptly to the call, Officer Hansen arrived at the house, ready to address the homeowners' distressing situation. The residents detailed an alarming sequence of events. While peacefully situated in their living room, an unidentified person abruptly burst into the back door, creating an immediate sense of vulnerability. To understand the intrusion, the homeowners swiftly investigated, only to find the premises devoid of any apparent intruders.

The unsettling episode didn't conclude there. Later, the homeowners, still rattled by the incident, glimpsed a mysterious, shadowy figure outside their back window. This unnerving observation heightened their anxiety, prompting them to seek the assistance of law enforcement, suspecting a potential break-in. Recognizing the gravity of the situation, Officer Hansen meticulously combed through the yard and the perimeter of the property, methodically searching for any traces of intruders. Despite his thorough inspection, no evidence of unauthorized individuals was found.

Taking every precaution, Officer Hansen, having secured the immediate safety of the homeowners, conscientiously finalized essential paperwork. Acknowledging the potential threat posed by the mysterious figure, he tactically stationed himself outside their home. This precautionary step wasn't just about averting a possible return of the enigmatic individual; it also functioned as a comforting presence for the anxious homeowners, restoring a sense of security in the aftermath of the unsettling events.

Officer Hansen focused on his laptop in his patrol car when an eerie sensation tingled down his spine, suggesting an unseen observer. Glancing out, he half-expected to find a figure looming by the driver's side door, yet the space was vacant. Resuming his work, a peculiar sound diverted his attention to the nearby house. It was just a cat rustling in a garbage can, to his relief.

Amid a moment of self-amusement, as he chuckled and returned his gaze to the laptop, a movement caught his eye. A shadowy figure emerged from behind a tree, stealthily traversing from the car's passenger side, across the hood, and towards the driver's side. Just as Officer Hansen poised to investigate, a sharp pop echoed, and the cruiser's window shattered. Bewilderingly, no one was in sight.

Convinced that his dash cam might have captured the perpetrator, Officer Hansen eagerly retrieved images on his phone. As he watched, the shadow, detached from any identifiable figure, advanced to the front of the car. Strangely, as if a finger had obscured the lens, the screen went black briefly. Once the obstruction cleared, it revealed the aftermath of the shattered window. This unsettling sequence deeply unnerved Officer Hansen, prompting him to share the eerie footage with his Sergeant. The experience left him so rattled that he promptly requested to be relieved from that particular watch.

Following these events, the precinct received numerous reports about the mysterious shadow. Despite the mounting calls, Officer Hansen attributed the phenomena to witches rather than ghosts, perhaps finding a more grounded explanation for the inexplicable occurrences.

Haunted Crossroads

Officer Tony Hansen found himself tangled in the enigmatic shadows of Salem, a man grounded in reason thrust into the realm of the inexplicable. As peculiar events unfolded, he balanced on the precipice between rationality and the supernatural, questioning the very essence of his reality.

Eerie encounters, once dismissed as mere folklore, now clung to him like the persistent fog on

Salem's cobblestone streets. The whispers of witches and the unseen ballet of shadows wove a fresh narrative during his nightly patrols.

Yet, in the perplexing unknown, clarity proved elusive, and reason often yielded to the eerie allure of the supernatural. Officer Hansen, formerly a stalwart guardian of order, now stood at the crossroads where the logical intersected with the otherworldly.

As shadows persisted in their mysterious dance through Salem's haunted history, we bid farewell to Officer Hansen, an unwilling witness to the peculiar, forever haunted by the echoes of that fateful night. In Salem's twilight zone, where reality blurs and nightmares materialize, the boundary between law enforcer and mystic dissolves into the obscurity of darkness.

7

THE LANDLORD

ON A CHILLING NIGHT WITHIN THE CONFINES of an old doctor's office, Officers Jessica Rodriguez and Ryan Chang embarked on a perplexing journey. The tranquility of the halls was shattered by a jarring alarm, thrusting the officers into a world teeming with unforeseen challenges and eerie occurrences.

As they ventured further, the boundary between the living and the dead blurred, unsettling ordinary surroundings. Locked doors swung open of their own accord, strange sounds permeated the air, and an otherworldly presence seemed to guide the officers.

Brace yourself for a night where the strange unfolds, enveloping Officers Jessica Rodriguez and Ryan Chang in a narrative that transcends our understanding. Welcome to the enigmatic realm known as 'The Landlord.'

Disruptive Alarm

As the night unfolded, a disruptive alarm reverberated through the corridors of an aged doctor's office and an adjacent pharmacy. Dispatch promptly summoned Officer Jessica Rodriguez and Officer Ryan Chang to the scene, responding to a mysterious trigger causing a disturbance in an upstairs office. With the timely arrival of the landlord, the officers aimed to secure the premises but encountered an unforeseen obstacle. The landlord, unable to unlock the stairwell door, challenged Officer Rodriguez and Officer Chang to reach the upper levels. Despite their determined efforts, the obstacle persisted, prompting the officers to explore alternative means to access the second floor and identify the source of the alarm.

Upon arrival, the officers, opting for the elevator to access the second floor, were greeted by a dimly lit hallway. The sole source of light emanated from a fixture at the far end. Adhering to protocol, they systematically checked each door, finding everything seemingly secure. Upon reaching the last office, the landlord unlocked the door, allowing the officers to enter cautiously. Their inspection revealed an unused office space. Opening another door, they discovered a spacious waiting room and reception area with ten to twelve examination rooms, all clear. Satisfied that everything was in order, the officers proceeded to leave.

As Officers Rodriguez and Chang exited the office, a sense of unease settled in. It became apparent to Officer Rodriguez that the previously dim light guiding their way had been turned off. In its place, a closer light near the elevators illuminated the area. Officer Rodriguez noticed a sudden change in the demeanor of her squad mate, Officer Chang, who appeared visibly disturbed. Regarding the cause, Officer Rodriguez was asked: "Are you sure all the doors we checked were closed and locked?" Confirming they were, Officer Chang revealed that, strangely, every door they had recently secured was wide open. A wave of terror gripped both officers.

With persistent determination, the officers systematically secured and cleared each office. A sigh of relief swept over them upon completing the final office, seemingly resolving the situation. However, as they neared the main exit, poised to turn the corner into the waiting area, the door abruptly slammed shut behind them. At that moment, a disconcerting medley of strange noises and static feedback echoed from both officers' radios. "Now I just wanted to get out of there," the officer added, urgency tainting their voice.

Officers Jessica Rodriguez and Ryan Chang descended to the first floor, acknowledging the owner's absence and stressing the importance of reaching out before departure. In their attempt to contact the landlord, they called dispatch for a callback number to communicate their findings.

Dispatch assured that the owner was on the way and anticipated arrival within the next five minutes.

Mysterious Impostor

Baffled by the situation, the officers expressed their confusion to dispatch, insisting they had contacted the landlord earlier that night. Despite their certainty, the dispatcher contradicted their account, asserting that such communication with the landlord was implausible. According to the dispatcher, the alarm company had just contacted the landlord, adding more mystery to the situation. The officers needed clarification, grappling with the discrepancy between their understanding of the situation with the landlord and the information provided by dispatch.

Upon the arrival of the actual landlord, he expressed curiosity about the person who claimed to be the authorized landlord and had allowed the officers entry into the building. In an unexpected turn, the man clarified that the officers' description coincided with that of a doctor who had previously worked on the second floor — the same area they had just thoroughly searched. The irony deepened as it was revealed that this doctor had recently taken his own life at home just days before the strange incident unfolded. The revelation added a layer of unsettling mystery, leaving the officers grappling with the bizarre circumstance of being seemingly guided by a deceased individual through the premises.

Officers Jessica Rodriguez and Ryan Chang continued to be mystified, grappling with the perplexity of how the deceased man could have granted them access to the building. As a result, the two officers have deliberately chosen to avoid revisiting the unsettling office building.

Realm of the Unknown

Beneath the eerie moonlight, Officers Jessica Rodriguez and Ryan Chang found themselves entangled in a supernatural enigma within a peculiar office building. Guided by the spectral presence of a deceased doctor, they navigated through dim corridors, unlocking doors that separated the realms of the living and the departed.

As the mysterious events unfolded, the officers realized that the peculiar voice on their radios, the autonomously opening doors, and the cryptic instructions were all orchestrated by a ghostly presence. The supposed landlord, it turned out, was a departed soul, adding an extra layer of peculiarity to the already bizarre night.

Caught between the realms of the living and the dead, Officers Rodriguez and Chang were left with more questions than answers. The events within the aged office building transformed into a haunting narrative, underscoring the delicate boundary between the living and the deceased.

Opting to heed the warnings of the supernatural, they pledged to steer clear of the mysterious building that served as a bridge between worlds. In the realm of the unknown, some mysteries are best left untouched. The ghostly echoes of that night lingered in their minds, serving as a haunting reminder of the fragile separation between the living and the dead. And thus, our tale concludes—a chilling chapter in the enigmatic stories of the unexplained.

8
CORNER HOUSE

VENTURING DEEP INTO THE HEART of a small town cloaked in winter's icy embrace, Officer Trevor Davis, a vigilant night guardian, silently patrolled the snow-covered streets. On a tranquil night, Officer Davis encountered a mystery that could give even the most courageous individuals reason to hesitate. Within the seemingly abandoned house, secrets murmured through its dusty halls. Undeterred, our intrepid officer delved into the unknown, unraveling a strange encounter that changed his life forever.

Prepare yourself for "The Corner House" – a narrative intricately woven with shadows, echoes, and the profound reverberations of the unexplainable, unfolding against the tranquil canvas of a winter night in Nebraska.

The Abandoned House

On a frigid winter night in Nebraska, Officer Trevor Davis initiated his customary patrol, traversing the quiet streets with purpose. The town, draped in a snowy quilt, showcased scattered abandoned houses against the backdrop of a serene landscape. In the face of a notable surge in copper theft driven by escalating prices, the local police keenly observed a rise in stealing from the copper plumbing of these vacant homes. Acknowledging the pressing nature of the situation, the police underscored the indispensability of regular patrols as a strategic measure to thwart the theft of these valuable pipes.

In their unwavering dedication to safeguarding the community, Officer Davis and his fellow officers committed themselves to counteract the escalating menace of copper theft. Their strategy involved maintaining persistent vigilance throughout the town's wintry nights, ensuring a proactive and robust presence to deter potential thieves and protect the valuable infrastructure of the community.

Footsteps in Dust

During Officer Davis's patrol through the neighborhoods that night, his attention was drawn by a large two-story corner house. The house's side door, easily seen from the street, was wide open—something Officer Davis wouldn't have missed during his first patrol in the area. This noticeable entrance on the visible side of the big two-story building hinted that someone might have gotten in while Officer Davis was patrolling elsewhere. A strong feeling that something was wrong motivated him to investigate the situation.

The officer carefully searched for signs of intruders around the open door, checking for footprints, damage to the house, and any indications of someone still inside. After a prompt call to keep the station informed, he decided to inspect inside the house. Unease lingered as he approached the vacant home on that chilly night. Despite a thorough check, no footprints were found around the perimeter, dismissing any signs of breaking and entering. Upon entering, Officer Davis was met with a profound emptiness that enveloped the dwelling.

The officer scanned the room with his flashlight, exposing torn-down walls and scattered plaster across various places. Carefully inspecting the floor for any signs of footprints, he discovered none. Despite the disarray, there were no discernible signs of a break-in. The officer pondered, considering possibilities such as the force of the wind or a poorly secured door.

After ensuring everything was in order within the house, he started to leave. But right before he could exit, a notable thump resonated from the upper floor, joined by the contagious laughter of children. In that fleeting moment, he stopped, his senses alert. Urgently, he called out, directing the unseen children to descend without delay, intrigued and wary of the mysterious commotion echoing through the building.

Door to the Unknown

The house now descended into an unsettling quietness, prompting Officer Davis to urgently report "possible intruders" on his radio. He proceeded cautiously and moved through the dwelling, concentrating on the staircase leading to the upper floor. Taking deliberate steps, he scanned for any possible overlooked footprints and halted at the occasional sounds of children playing in the distance. Even though his calls received only silence, doubt seeped in, leading him to question the reliability of his hearing. Contemplating the idea that the disturbance might be just an animal or an open window upstairs, Officer Davis remained unfazed. He ascended the creaky staircase, his flashlight illuminating the otherwise silent expanse of the house.

Upon reaching the pinnacle of the staircase, the officer took a moment to survey the surroundings. Three bedrooms stood before him – one to the right, one to the left, and one straight ahead – each with closed doors. In that instant, he recollected catching only the faint sounds of the wind outside; other than that, the house was unsettlingly silent. Moving forward, he opted to test the right door first. Upon entering the room, he abruptly stopped, startled by the unmistakable thud from the bedroom to his left.

Attracted by the sound, he casually moved towards the door, his hand steadying on the handle. With careful intent, he turned the handle, swinging the door open. A beam of light from his flashlight cut through the darkness, unveiling the room's features as he cast a discerning gaze.

The room revealed its emptiness to Officer Davis, featuring only a small heap of dirt and plaster at its center. As he prepared to leave, an unexpected sight grabbed his attention – a piece of paper delicately resting on the debris pile. Intrigued, he moved closer, intensifying his focus on this find. He picked up the carefully positioned torn page, revealing an image of a police officer torn from an old children's book.

The situation was oddly strange. The discovery of that piece of paper felt like too much of a coincidence for Officer Davis. Feeling chills running down his back, he released the torn paper and quickly inspected the remaining rooms before exiting the house. That night, the dwelling seemed devoid of life, leaving a lasting impact on Officer Davis. This experience played a role in his decision to avoid revisiting the unsettling home in the future.

Photograph's Haunting Tale

On a frosty night in the serene, snow-covered town, Officer Trevor Davis embarked on his patrol, oblivious to the mystery awaiting him in the cold expanse of Nebraska. As he cautiously entered a vacant two-story house, the echoes of children's laughter played illusions on his senses. The lifeless rooms concealed untold secrets, leading him to an unsettling discovery on the creaky staircase—a home adorned only with dirt, plaster, and a peculiar, weathered photograph.

The torn image depicted a haunting scene—a police officer resembling Officer Davis, extracted from the pages of an ancient children's book. This chilling revelation whispered a connection to the past through the silent corridors of the desolate house. With the eerie encounter engraved in his mind, Officer Davis heeded the warning conveyed by the unsettling silence. He reported the otherworldly discovery, leaving the enigmatic house untouched, its secrets interred in the cold night.

The once lively dwelling now stands in an eerie hush, a testament to the inexplicable. Officer Davis carries with him the chilling reminder that, at times, the quietest corners conceal the darkest mysteries.

9

THE NIGHT WATCH

DIVE INTO THE VIBRANT SPIRIT OF OKLAHOMA, where the walls of a children's hospital resonate with timeless tales that span across the ages. Within its healing embrace lies a sanctuary for the young and a repository of stories echoing through time—a narrative woven with threads of resilience, compassion, and enigmatic whispers that linger within its sacred halls.

In this town, the past intertwines seamlessly with the present, and a beacon of hope guards secrets untold. However, caution accompanies this venture, for as we delve into the mysteries of a hospital with a spectral reputation, you may find yourself teetering on the brink of disbelief, questioning the elusive boundary between the living and the unknown.

So, gather close, my curious companions, as we

embark on a voyage into the realm of ethereal murmurs, ready to unveil the secrets veiled in the shadows of the children's hospital in the heart of Oklahoma.

Resilient Sanctuary

Situated in the heart of Oklahoma's city center, the children's hospital stands as a symbol of resilience and compassion, surrounded by the echoes of an industrial past. With roots reaching back several decades, this institution has weathered the storms of time, extending its nurturing embrace even through the hardships of the Great Depression. It has become an integral part of the town, not merely as a medical facility but as a living chronicle of unwavering dedication to the well-being of the community's youngest members.

The hospital's significance goes beyond its role as a healthcare provider; it has evolved into a central hub for the townsfolk. Its halls echo with children's laughter and the hum of dedicated medical professionals working tirelessly to improve their young patients' lives. The hospital's pioneering Pediatric Cancer Research has contributed to medical advancements and brought well-deserved recognition to the facility.

Behind the scenes, the city has demonstrated a commitment to the hospital's upkeep, wisely utilizing public tax dollars. This financial support ensures that the hospital remains a historical symbol and a modern, well-equipped haven for healing. The mayor, recognizing the hospital's vital role, has taken proactive steps to enhance security. A collaboration between the City's Police Department and the hospital has resulted in a carefully crafted agreement, ensuring a constant vigil to safeguard the well-being of those within the hospital walls, day and night.

Red Ribbons

Despite the town's overall safety, the hospital naturally transforms into a haven for those in need, including occasional unwanted visitors. The compassionate hospital staff, fully aware of their caregiving role, extends a helping hand to these wanderers, showcasing the institution's dedication to care and community ties. Through a mix of history, medical progress, and community support, the children's hospital stands as a powerful symbol of hope and healing in the heart of Oklahoma.

The young patients at the hospital faced various illnesses, but the dedicated staff ensured they received excellent care. During the Great Depression, children with terminal diseases had red ribbons tied to their beds' ends as a precaution for evacuation. This practice helped nurses identify those requiring special attention during transport. Although many once life-threatening diseases are now curable, the use of these ribbons ceased. Over time, they acquired a perceived negative energy.

Recently, the hospital underwent extensive

renovations thanks to a substantial Federal Grant. Consequently, the Cancer Ward's young occupants were relocated a floor below, and the area was sealed off. The upper floor became quiet during the night to avoid disturbing resting children due to ongoing construction. Concerns arose about potential access to the renovated area, leading the staff to worry about children or intruders sneaking in at night. In response, the Police Department deployed an officer to patrol the floors, ensuring the safety of the hospital and its renovated spaces.

Spectral Whispers

A recent addition to the police force, Officer Avery Simon embraced his role enthusiastically, finding deep satisfaction in shouldering the responsibility of the night watch at the hospital. Night after night, Officer Simon went beyond the call of duty, establishing a heartwarming connection with the young residents of the medical facility. His presence became a source of comfort for the children, a reassuring constant before he ascended the stairs to maintain a vigilant watch over the closed-off floor.

On a specific night, after completing his second round around the secured area, Officer Simon's sharp senses picked up the faint sound of tiny footsteps echoing down the silent hallway. Intrigued and attentive, he swiftly turned to investigate the mysterious occurrence, only to be met with an eerie emptiness—no visible presence, no discernible footprints even in the settled dust. The inexplicable incident left Officer Simon puzzled, deepening the enigma surrounding his nightly duties at the hospital.

Disregarding the peculiar incident, Officer Simon pressed on with his vigilant patrol. However, laughter echoed across the hall as he exited the room. Suspecting that one of the children may have trailed behind him, he entered the room genially, aiming not to disrupt their tranquility. Much to his astonishment, upon entering the room, he was met with an emptiness that held no evidence of anyone's recent presence. The laughter, now untraceable, added an additional layer of mystery to the unfolding events, leaving Officer Simon both intrigued and perplexed.

Expecting a brief break, Officer Simon headed towards the exit to grab a coffee. However, as he approached the stairwell, the sound of a door shutting reached his ears. Instinctively, he pivoted around, fixing his gaze down the hallway, where he discerned subtle movement. To his bewilderment, a small red ribbon was seen gliding across the center of the hallway floor. A sense of unease creeping over him, Officer Simon cautiously retreated from the area and promptly informed the nurse on duty, who, in turn, was visibly unnerved by the occurrence.

The following day, Officer Simon, still wrestling with the unsettling events of the previous night, formally requested to be relieved from his watch duty. The haunting notion of lost souls wandering through the renovated floor deeply unsettled him despite understanding that the children had no malicious intentions. Ultimately, Officer Simon, unable to shake off the lingering unease, made the resolute decision never to return to that specific duty post. In doing so, he left behind an unspoken yet palpable sense of mystery and apprehension, concluding the enigmatic chapter of his night patrols at the hospital.

Abandoned Watch

Officer Avery Simon, a watchful guardian in the shadows, unraveled mysteries within the heart of healing. Once a haven of hope, the resilient sanctuary now hid secrets in its quiet corridors, escaping mortal understanding.

Simon's dedicated watch, meant for protection, became a journey through echoes of a bygone era. Red ribbons, once comforting symbols for children, now floated, telling tales of an enduring past. Laughter echoed, footsteps danced, and an unsettling emptiness embraced the night.

Opting to abandon his post, the officer's departure left the hospital's history unchanged. A chapter closed, yet the mystery lingered in the sacred halls. The fortified sanctuary, concealing countless stories within renovated spaces and sealed-off secrets, resembled a ghostly treasure chest. Thus, Officer Avery Simon's enigmatic night patrols concluded, leaving behind the lingering question: What untold tales still whisper in the quiet corners of the children's hospital in the heart of Oklahoma?

10

THE LIGHTHOUSE

PICTURE THE BREATHTAKING coastal landscape of North Carolina, adorned with impressive lighthouses that stand as sentinels of history and beauty. Once vital guides for sailors navigating treacherous waters, these towering structures now beckon tourists, vividly narrating the maritime tales etched into the region's soul.

Some legendary lighthouses, guardians of seafaring journeys, have been carefully relocated to preserve their rich history. Their lights once beacons guiding ships through dangerous waters, now illuminate stories of resilience and change. Tourists flock to witness these majestic structures standing tall against the vast expanse of the Atlantic Ocean.

Yet, amid the enduring beacons that dot the coastline, one lighthouse harbors a tale of sorrow.

This lighthouse, once a symbol of safety and maritime triumph, now stands closed to the public. It ceased its duty after a harrowing incident, a chilling chapter involving a police officer entangled in the enigmatic web of the supernatural. In this narrative, we embark on a journey into the shadows of this desolate structure, where reality and the unknown intertwine in a dance that lingers, steadfastly refusing to fade away.

The Lighthouse

The incident unfolded on a night resonating with maritime legends carried by coastal winds, shrouded in mystery and sorrow. Though the details are unclear, it's said that the isolated lighthouse witnessed a confrontation that changed its fate. A police officer, there to protect, became involved in events leading to the lighthouse's closure.

The Arcadia Lighthouse, historically a pivotal beacon along the coastline, held paramount significance. With Arcadia Island posing a concealed hazard to passing ships navigating the waterways, numerous incidents of vessels running aground prompted the town to take action. Subsequently, a lighthouse was constructed to alleviate the risks of the island's obscurity during the nighttime. The diligent keepers of the lighthouse assumed the crucial responsibility of ensuring the continuous illumination of the candles that amplified the signal for incoming vessels, particularly during the challenging hurricane season, thus safeguarding maritime traffic from potential dangers.

Advancing several decades into the future, the Historical Foundation strategically relocated the lighthouse inland. Evolving technological advancements in navigation had rendered the lighthouse obsolete for its original purpose, transforming it into a sought-after tourist attraction. Visitors now had the opportunity to ascend to the structure's pinnacle, gaining insights into the lighthouse's inner workings and exploring its keepers' erstwhile living quarters.

Yet, on a radiant June day, the residents were startled to witness a woman adorned in a nightgown strolling toward the lighthouse. Tourists exchanged curious glances as she ascended the stairs, eventually reaching the summit. Little did anyone anticipate that her actions would catalyze a chain of events leading to the permanent closure of the lighthouse. Instead of just exploring, the woman approached the railings, stretched her arms solemnly, and perpetrated a shocking leap from the lighthouse, descending to the unyielding cement ground below.

Eyewitnesses to the incident speculated that the woman might have been under some form of possession, noting the unsettling detail that her pupils appeared as white as snow and she remained unresponsive to calls from onlookers. Subsequent revelations by the Police unveiled a troubling truth: the woman was an escaped mental patient from the nearby inland hospital. Regardless of the circumstances, the tragic death of the woman left an indelible mark on the collective memory of many spectators who bore witness to that sweltering June day.

In the ensuing years, the lighthouse remained a prime tourist attraction. Responding to past incidents of vandalism, the Lighthouse Historical Society proactively addressed the issue by installing surveillance cameras. Alongside these measures, a poignant remembrance plaque was placed, paying tribute to the woman who had tragically ended her own life. Following these initiatives, a sense of tranquility enveloped the lighthouse, fostering an atmosphere of quiet reflection.

Ward's Encounter

A native of the Outer Banks, June Ward, a young officer with the local Police, had spent her entire life in the coastal region. Initially, she had only heard in passing about the tragic incident involving the girl who took her own life, giving it minimal consideration. However, her perspective shifted when the local Historical Society approached the Police requesting nighttime surveillance around the lighthouse. This directive was issued by a string of break-ins afflicting the area, coupled with the enigmatic malfunctioning of surveillance cameras, hinting at potential interference with the lenses.

Embracing the responsibility of the night shift, Officer Ward found solace in the town's nocturnal tranquility, characterized by subdued tourists. Eager to fulfill the request from the Lighthouse Historical Society, she commenced her night duties by conducting a thorough inspection of the premises, diligently examining the doors for any signs of tampering. The Society had entrusted her with keys to access the interior if necessary. In light of the consistent pattern of incidents reported just before dawn each day, Officer Ward remained steadfast in her commitment to be at the lighthouse during those crucial moments.

The rest of Officer Ward's rounds transpired without any incidents, and she soon reached the lighthouse just as the sun started to cast its glow over the horizon. After parking her vehicle, she stepped out and began a walk around the perimeter, finding nothing awry. Nevertheless, an unforeseen twist transpired as Officer Ward, positioned beside the secured door, discerned the unmistakable sound of crying from within the lighthouse. Acting instinctually, she swiftly retrieved the keys and swung the door open. Much to her surprise, no one greeted her sight. Undeterred, she ventured into the keyholder quarters, scanning for any telltale signs, only to abruptly halt her investigation upon hearing the subtle creaking of stairs.

Ascending the lighthouse stairs with deliberate

caution, Officer Ward called out to whoever was inside, urging them to come down promptly. A brief pause ensued as she traversed the hatch leading to the deck. She encountered a woman adorned in a flowing, floral nightgown who stood fixated, exuding an unmistakable sense of distress. Reacting swiftly, Officer Ward discreetly drew her gun and, in a calm tone, addressed the woman.

"Ma'am," she whispered, concern etched across her face. "Are you okay? Do you need help?"

The woman maintained a silent pause, her gaze unyielding, before pivoting and climbing onto the edge of the lighthouse. Approaching cautiously, Officer Ward extended her hand toward the woman's dress. A sudden chill enveloped her chest as the woman seized her arm. Officer Ward recoiled, feeling a cold sensation, and observed the pallid eyes and terrifying expression on the woman's face. Without warning, the woman plunged over the lighthouse's edge, eliciting Officer Ward's anguished cry. "No!" she shouted, rushing to the precipice only to find a space below.

The enigmatic woman had seemingly disappeared into thin air. Descending the stairs with urgency, Officer Ward left the lighthouse and stared up at the space where the woman had been. Distressed, she radioed the station, urgently seeking the immediate assistance of The Lighthouse Historical Society. The crucial task was to review the surveillance tapes and unravel the unsettling events.

Upon the woman's arrival, Officer Ward recounted the perplexing encounter. The woman, visibly astonished, swiftly retrieved the tapes for Officer Ward. Despite multiple viewings, each attempt to reveal the elusive girl on the video ended in a frustrating blank screen. Observing the blistered skin on Officer Ward's arm, the woman turned to a framed picture on the mantle.

"Is this the girl?" she inquired.

As Officer Ward examined the old black-and-white photos, she was startled to find the unmistakable image of the girl she had encountered.

"Yes," Ward affirmed.

"That's the girl who took her own life several years ago," the woman solemnly disclosed.

As Officer Ward departed from the lighthouse that day, she sensed the imminent closure of the structure. Surprisingly, the tower was bulldozed a year later to pave the way for a park. Nevertheless, even today, tales endure of a young girl in a nightgown gracefully strolling through the park — an eerie reminder of a tragic tale that persists in the collective memory.

Ward's Ghostly Embrace

As the sun sets on this chapter of maritime mystery and spectral encounters, we bid farewell to the Arcadia Lighthouse. This beacon once guided ships through treacherous waters but is now condemned to the shadows of the unknown.

Officer June Ward, a guardian of the night, was entangled in a web of inexplicable events transcending the realms of the living. A ghostly figure clad in a flowing nightgown led her on a macabre dance between reality and the supernatural.

The Lighthouse Historical Society, with its surveillance tapes and chilling revelations, tried to grasp the fleeting specter haunting the lighthouse. Yet, the ghostly maiden defied capture, leaving nothing but a shiver down Officer Ward's spine and a haunting emptiness.

As the bulldozers roared to life, reducing the once-hallowed structure to rubble, one can't help but wonder if the spirits lingering within found solace or if they now wander, untethered, through the whispers of the wind.

A tranquil park may replace the Arcadia Lighthouse, but the echoes of that fateful night persist. Visitors speak of a spectral presence—a young girl in a nightgown, strolling gracefully through the park's pathways. Is it a ghostly apparition or a lingering memory etched into the very fabric of the land?

In the twilight of this tale, we're left to ponder the mysteries that endure, the shadows that linger, and the whispers that persist. Such is the way of the unknown, my friends, where reality and the supernatural entwine in a dance that transcends the boundaries of time.

So, as you tread cautiously through the corridors of your existence, beware the unseen, for in the darkness, the echoes of the Arcadia Lighthouse may still reverberate, reminding us that some stories, no matter how buried, refuse to be extinguished.

11

PHANTOM FROLICKER

IN THE UNYIELDING RAIN AND SHROUDED in the enigma of the unknown, we explore the desolate lands of Western Nebraska. In this realm, storms are feared by those who inhabit their shadows. Officer Joey Cross, familiar with the nightly routine, experiences an unsettling twist during a night that seemed initially calm as storms bring more than mere rain. Join us as we unravel the mystery beneath the thunderous skies—a narrative of shadows, apparitions, and lingering memories. Welcome to the eerie saga of Officer Joey Cross and the Phantom Frolicker.

The Eerie Farmhouse

The storms, despised by everyone in Western Nebraska, cast a relentless shadow on Officer Joey Cross. As the on-duty cop, he faced an unending series of challenges beneath the downpours that seemed never to let up. Cross began his nightshift rounds on a typical rainy night, hoping for a tranquil patrol. The late hours usually unfolded without incident, promising a quiet watch.

However, roughly two hours into his evening shift, the radio burst to life with a sudden crackle. A solitary elderly lady living alone in a farmhouse on the outskirts of town urgently reported a strange occurrence: a young girl frolicking in her backyard. Officer Cross, resigned to getting soaked, headed towards the house.

Pulling into the lengthy driveway, a shiver ran up Cross's arms, prompting a gentle tap on the brakes as a thick mist drifted across the path. With its creaky shutters and weathered roof, the house resembled something out of a horror movie. Despite the eerie atmosphere, Officer Cross parked the car, cringing at the intermittent flashes of lightning illuminating the sky. The unfolding events hinted at a night far from the quiet watch he had initially anticipated.

Vanishing Specter

Dashing to the porch, Officer Cross shook the rain from his hat before approaching the front door. A thunderous clap echoed through the Nebraska sky just as the older woman swung the door open, peering at the officer. Relief washed over her as she recognized him and swiftly invited him inside. Glancing around the dusty old house, Officer Cross realized the lady must live alone. She appeared a bit frightened, but given the storm outside, fear seemed almost inevitable.

The lady spotted a little girl darting among the trees in her backyard. Officer Cross walked to the back sliding door, peering into the darkness. The clouds veiled the moon, casting the yard into pitch-black obscurity. Even with sporadic flashes of lightning, he couldn't discern any signs of anyone. Cracking the door open, he shone his flashlight around the yard, still finding no trace. Just as he was leaving, a gasp caught his attention from behind.

"She's there!" the old lady yelled. "She's in the house!"

Officer Cross spun around abruptly, seizing a glimpse of a pink floral dress vanishing around the corner. Questions raced through his mind – how did she slip past him, and why wasn't she wet? With a quick jog, Cross rounded the corner just as the young girl turned, an eerie giggle lingering in the air. Suddenly, she vanished before his eyes.

Perplexed, he rubbed his face, uncertain about what had just occurred when the old lady called out again.

"There!" she pointed. "She's outside again!"

Officer Cross hurried to the door and observed the little girl skipping into the field, vanishing into the fog. Tugging the hood of his rain jacket over his head, Officer Cross ventured into the area. Despite hours of searching, there was no sign of the little girl. Eventually, after reassuring the woman that nobody was there, Officer Cross returned to the police precinct, baffled by the strange events that had just unfolded.

Months drifted by without a whisper, and after the elderly lady's passing, a new family took residence in the old farmhouse on the town's outskirts. Then, on a stormy night, Officer Cross, now on duty, received a call from the same house about the reappearance of the little girl. This time, however, he passed the call to someone else, unable to shake the haunting memories of the thick fog and the enigmatic little girl.

Eternal Enigma

Officer Joey Cross was entangled in a puzzling mystery that defied logical explanation. Storms, silent keepers of secrets, murmured tales that transcended the realm of the living. The aged farmhouse on the outskirts harbored enigmas that straddled the line between reality and the otherworldly.

Memories of the haunting experience clung to Officer Cross like a lingering ghost, resisting the passage into forgetfulness. Even the demise of the elderly lady failed to quell the mysteries residing in the shadowy confines of the house. Unaware of the spectral echoes, a new, unsuspecting family moved in, only to unearth the same eerie enigma on a stormy night.

Now an unwilling observer, Officer Cross handed over the case to another, unable to confront the phantoms lurking in the misty fields. The elusive little girl continued her unexplained appearances, leaving behind a trail of unanswered questions. Ultimately, the farmhouse stood as a cryptic monument, its secrets wrapped in the thunderous echoes of storms, a chilling testament to the unexplainable and the eerie.

12

CASINO ENCOUNTER

THE MENTION OF "CALIFORNIA" EVOKES images of sand, surf, sun, and bathing suits. Journeying northward from the glamour of celebrity homes leads to a different landscape. In these deserts, summer days seem endless, and treeless plains provide little shelter from the scorching sun.

In the sun-drenched deserts of northern California, a story unfolds about Native American heritage grappling with the challenges of progress. The government allocates vast areas to indigenous tribes, sparking a clash between tradition and the pursuit of prosperity. As the sun sets, an unexpected turn occurs—sacred and mundane elements collide, giving rise to casinos in the arid soil, seamlessly integrating into daily life.

Amid the sounds of casino construction at night, protests arise against the encroachment on sacred land. However, the enthusiasm dwindles with time, replaced by an eerie calm disrupted by tangible and spectral shadows.

Officer Lonnie Howell patrols in the nocturnal casino ambiance, witnessing something elusive — a disconcerting mystery in his memories. Brace yourself, for the shadows of the past, have a peculiar way of infiltrating the present.

Tribal Disillusionment

Bathed in the golden glow of the northern Californian sun, the vast deserts become a canvas upon which the intricate threads of Native American culture are woven. Here, amidst the relentless heat, the government allocates expansive stretches of land to these indigenous tribes. However, the harsh conditions render agriculture impractical, leading the communities to grapple with preserving their heritage in a landscape unforgiving to traditional livelihoods.

Amidst this struggle, a surprising resilience takes root as casinos emerge, unexpectedly intertwining with the fabric of daily life. These establishments become more than just economic ventures; they connect livelihoods while attempting to preserve the rich cultural tapestry threatened by the barren surroundings.

However, against this backdrop of cultural preservation, a troubling turn of events unfolds. In 2010, the government seized a large piece of land and put it up for auction, letting the highest bidder take control. Even though the tribes earnestly made their case, providing evidence of cultural artifacts and sacred burial sites on the property, their appeals were ignored by the government's single-minded pursuit of financial gains, overshadowing the calls for cultural preservation.

The stewardship of this land is then handed over to a wealthy oil tycoon whose ambitions extend beyond the black gold beneath the earth. Eager to capitalize on the booming casino industry, the tycoon becomes the new custodian of this contested territory, further exacerbating the clash between tradition and profit-driven motives.

Throughout the construction phase of the casino, impassioned protests emanated from the tribes, fervently opposing the encroachment on their cultural heritage. However, over time, the enthusiasm of the opposition dwindled as local Native Americans came to a disheartening realization of the irreparable harm inflicted upon their ancestral land. Several years later, the same affluent businessman extended his business operations into the previously untouched segment of the confiscated territory.

Unfortunately, it was discovered that the entire region was designated as Native American burial grounds. Upon learning about the proposed development, this revelation sparked unrest among the residents, leading to protests that occasionally turned violent. To forestall any escalation, the casino maintained a constant vigil by deploying police officers around the clock. Assigned to this responsibility was Officer Lonnie Howell, a lifelong resident familiar with the local tribes. He willingly patrolled the casino during the third shift, enabling him to embrace the tranquility of the occasionally cool nights in the California desert.

Nocturnal Shadows

In the nocturnal ambiance of the casino, the interplay of light and shadow crafted obscure silhouettes at its rear. Officer Howell, savoring the serene desert atmosphere, often kept a vigilant eye on the rear entrance. In the quiet of the night, he believed he discerned enigmatic shadows on the railings near the roof, seemingly gazing beyond the hills. However, upon approaching, these spectral figures elusively dissipated. Intrigued, he shared his experiences with his fellow officers, who, in a jesting manner, whimsically conjectured that these ethereal shadows could be ancient spirits emanating from the burial grounds.

As Officer Howell continued his routine shifts in the following days, the community's discontent became increasingly noticeable. The reason for the unease became clear when Officer Howell found out that a company was planning to bulldoze an area thought to be an ancient Native American cemetery soon. The impending destruction of this sacred site fueled the collective frustration among the locals.

With rising tensions, the protests took an unexpected turn. Instead of expressing anger openly, the community voiced their dissent through prayer and song. The night air carried the captivating melodies of the desert, forming a unique symphony that blended both resistance and reverence. Officer Howell found himself deep in thought as he navigated the changing dynamics of the situation.

As the protestors slowly dispersed, Officer Howell decided to take one last walk before sunrise. His quiet stroll abruptly changed when he noticed shadowy figures on the balcony, silently observing the hills. Despite his attempts to engage them, the figures remained unmoved. Stepping forward with determination, Officer Howell firmly instructed them to come down immediately, emphasizing that they were not allowed on the property.

Upon hearing those words, one of the mysterious black figures turned toward Officer Howell and elegantly descended from the balcony, touching down several yards away. Shrouded in shadow, the figure fixed a menacing gaze directly upon him. Despite the obscured features, Officer Howell discerned what seemed to be the visage of an older Native American man. However, as he approached, the shadow swiftly evaded him, emitting a high-pitched scream that reverberated through the air. Accelerating in flight, the spectral figure hurtled towards Officer Howell, slamming into him and forcefully propelling him backward onto the ground.

Upon Officer Howell's return to the casino, a murmur of discussions surrounded sightings of an older Native American man and the booming resonance of his powerful scream. The scream reverberated so forcefully that it echoed throughout the entire expanse of the casino, leaving an indelible mark on the atmosphere. The lasting impression engraved in Officer Howell's mind was the enraged countenance of the Native American man, his face twisted with intense fury as he charged directly at him. The details of this furious visage remained vivid and haunting, persistently echoing in Officer Howell's thoughts.

Contrary to expectations, the casino continued its operations unabated in the aftermath, with rumors circulating about the persistent pursuit of their excavation plans. Officer Howell grappled with the haunting memory of the mysterious encounter, compelling him to swiftly distance himself from the unsettling atmosphere that had permeated the establishment. Fueled by a potent blend of fear and inexplicable events, he actively sought a new job, driven by the earnest desire to escape the pervasive shadows that seemed to envelop every nook and cranny of the casino. His unwavering decision never to return transcended professional considerations, symbolizing a deep-seated determination to bury the enigmatic incident in the annals of the past, forever shrouded in unsettling mystery. Since the shadowy attack, Officer Howell discovered solace in his new assignment, steadfastly refusing to revisit the eerie chapter of his past.

A Ghostly Grudge

Once a vigilant guardian in the quiet desert night, Officer Lonnie Howell was entangled in a mysterious dance with forces beyond understanding. The eerie echoes of that encounter stayed with him, sketching the ghostly outlines of an otherworldly grudge.

In the echoing corridors of the casino, where tradition clashed with profit, Officer Howell decided to break free from the oppressive grip of the casino's malevolent shadows. Yet, as he walked away, a lingering question remained: What secrets were hidden in the vast California desert? The ancient spirits, disturbed by relentless progress, now haunted every casino corner.

The determined pursuit of excavation plans persisted, with whispers of the angered Native American spirit carried by the desert winds. The casino, seemingly unaffected by the spectral vendetta, continued its operations with calculated indifference. Officer Howell's departure, a mere detail in the casino's grand scheme, left a sense of mystery and foreboding.

As the story unfolds, one must ponder – does the desert hold the key to unraveling past secrets? Or will the shadows endure, casting their ghostly shroud over the casino's affairs? Only time will reveal the enigmatic legacy of Lonnie Howell and the ancient spirits, angered by the violation of their resting grounds, that may forever haunt the golden embrace of the California desert.

CONCLUSION

AS WE BID FAREWELL to the cryptic tales woven within the Night Shift Chronicles, we find ourselves standing at the crossroads of reality and the unknown. These stories, like spectral whispers echoing through the corridors of our imagination, have not just scratched the surface but delved into the very soul of the inexplicable.

Picture the haunted hospital where brave souls patrolled the shadowed hallways, the Louisiana swamp with its secrets submerged in murky depths, and the church complex where ethereal shadows danced in the dim light. These narratives, each a testament to the human spirit confronting the supernatural, have left an indelible mark, an otherworldly tattoo on the skin of our collective consciousness.

No mere flights of fancy, these tales remind us that the paranormal is a relentless force, not confined to the realms of fiction but entwined with our tangible existence. The custodians of order, the sentinels of security, found themselves thrust into the abyss of the unexplainable, their lives forever altered, reshaped by encounters that defy the boundaries of anticipation.

As we stand on the precipice of concluding our journey through the Night Shift Chronicles, let it be known that the allure of the unknown is not just a passing fancy—it's a timeless fascination that transcends the skeptics' raised eyebrows. These stories, steeped in eerie encounters and unexplained phenomena, beckon us to peer into the abyss and reflect on the enduring mysteries that persist beyond the grasp of our mortal minds.

So, fellow travelers, whether you approached these tales with trepidation or fascination, remember that they have carved their niche in the expansive canvas of the inexplicable. Your companionship on this odyssey into the perplexing and otherworldly has been cherished and valued.

I extend a spectral hand as we part ways, inviting you to share your reflections through a review and rating. Your insights, dear listeners, are the lanterns guiding us through the shadows. Until our paths entwine again, may the night's mysteries intrigue and unsettle you. Here's to the anticipation of mysterious adventures in the dark corners of our imagination. Until next we meet, stay vigilant, stay curious, and let the unknown be your guide: goodnight and pleasant dreams in the realm of the unexplained.

www.ingramcontent.com/pod-product-compliance
Lightning Source LLC
Chambersburg PA
CBHW060536080526
44586CB00012B/752